GRADE
2

Success With

Writing

New York • Toronto • London • Auckland • Sydney
Mexico City • New Delhi • Hong Kong • Buenos Aires

Teaching *Resources*

State Standards Correlations

To find out how this book helps you meet your state's standards,
log on to **www.scholastic.com/ssw**

Written by Lisa Molengraft
Cover design by Ka-Yeon Kim-Li
Interior illustrations by Mark Mason
Interior design by Quack & Company

ISBN 978-0-545-20078-3

Introduction

One of the greatest challenges teachers and parents face is helping children develop independent writing skills. Each writing experience is unique and individualized, making it each child's responsibility to plan, expand, and proofread his or her work. However, the high-interest topics and engaging exercises in this book will both stimulate and encourage children as they develop the necessary skills to become independent writers. This book uses these strategies to introduce grade-appropriate skills that can be used in daily writing assignments such as journals, stories, and letters. Like a stepladder, this book will help children reach the next level of independent writing.

Table of Contents

You're Sharp!

 A sentence begins with a **capital letter**.

Circle the words that show the correct way to begin each sentence.

many Of
Many of
my friends are in second grade.

Our teacher
our Teacher
keeps a fish tank in our classroom.

The reading
the reading
center has many good books.

the globe
The globe
helps us find places around the world.

we Study
We study
about the weather.

Our class
our Class
won the reading contest.

Stick With It

 A sentence begins with a **capital letter.**

Write the beginning words correctly to make a sentence.

1.
art class _____ begins at noon.

2.
today we _____ are making clay pots.

3.
first, we _____ form the clay into balls.

4.
the next _____ step is to make a hole in
the ball.

5.
my teacher _____ dries the pots.

6.
next week _____ we will paint the pots.

A Whale of a Sentence

 A **telling sentence** *ends with a* **period** *(.).*

Rewrite the sentences using capital letters and periods.

1. the blue whale is the largest animal in the world

_____

2. even dinosaurs were not as large as the blue whale

_____

3. blue whales are not part of the fish family

_____

4. the blue whale has no teeth

_____

5. blue whales eat tiny sea creatures

_____

6. blue whales have two blowholes

_____

That Sounds Fishy to Me

 A **telling sentence** *begins with a* **capital letter** *and ends with a* **period**.

Write a sentence about each fish. Remember to tell a complete idea.

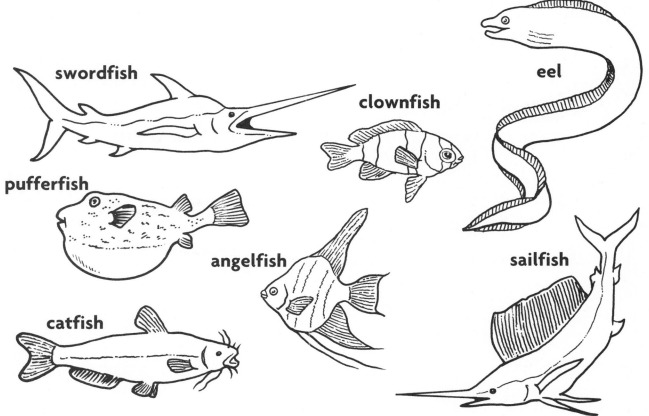

swordfish

clownfish

eel

pufferfish

angelfish

sailfish

catfish

1. The swordfish has a long snout.

2. _____

3. _____

4. _____

5. _____

6. _____

7. _____

Ask Mother Goose

A sentence that asks a question ends with a **question mark** *(?).*
It often begins with one of these words.

Who . . .	*Where . . .*	*Why . . .*	*Could . . .*
What . . .	*When . . .*	*Will . . .*	

Rewrite the questions using capital letters and
question marks.

1. where is the king's castle

_____

2. who helped Humpty Dumpty

_____

3. why did the cow jump over the moon

_____

4. will the frog become a prince

_____

5. could the three mice see

_____

Ask the Wolf

 *An **asking sentence** begins with a **capital letter** and ends with a **question mark** (?). It often begins with one of these words.*

How . . .	*Can . . .*	*Would . . .*
Did . . .	*Is . . .*	*Should . . .*

Imagine that you can meet the Big Bad Wolf. What questions would you ask him about Little Red Riding Hood and the Three Little Pigs? Use a different beginning word for each question you write.

1. How _____

2. Did _____

3. Can _____

1. Is _____

2. Should _____

3. Would _____

 Pretend that you are the Big Bad Wolf. Write sentences on another sheet of paper to answer each question above.

Is Your Head in the Clouds?

 *A **telling sentence** ends with a **period** (.).*
*An **asking sentence** ends with a **question mark** (?).*

Finish each sentence by putting a period or a question mark in
the cloud at the end.

1. Clouds can look like cotton balls, feathers, or blankets

2. Do you know what makes a cloud form in the sky

3. Have you ever seen dark clouds on rainy days

4. Dark clouds may bring thunderstorms

5. Can you imagine pictures in the clouds

6. White clouds drift across the blue sky

7. Why don't we see clouds every day

8. Rain, snow, sleet, and hail may fall from clouds

 **Find two telling sentences and two questions in one of your favorite books. Write them on
another sheet of paper.**

Sunny Sentences

*Every sentence begins with a **capital letter**.*
*A **telling sentence** ends with a **period** (.).*
*An **asking sentence** ends with a **question mark** (?).*

Rewrite each sentence correctly.

1. the sun is the closest star to Earth

_____

2. the sun is not the brightest star

_____

3. what is the temperature of the sun

_____

4. the sun is a ball of hot gas

_____

5. how large is the sun

_____

6. will the sun ever burn out

_____

On another sheet of paper, write a sentence with two mistakes. Ask a friend to circle the mistakes.

Camp Fiddlestick

 A telling sentence is called a **statement**. *An asking sentence is called a* **question**.
Now ask yourself:

How do sentences begin? How do statements end? How do questions end?

Write three statements and three questions about the picture.

Cabins →
← Stables

Statements:

1. _____

2. _____

3. _____

Questions:

1. _____

2. _____

3. _____

 Sing "Where is Thumbkin?" to yourself. Count the number of questions and statements in the song.

A Happy Camper

→ *Complete:*
Every sentence begins with a _____.
A statement ends with a _____.
A question ends with a _____.

Uh oh! Dalton was in a hurry when he wrote this letter. Help him find 10 mistakes. Circle them.

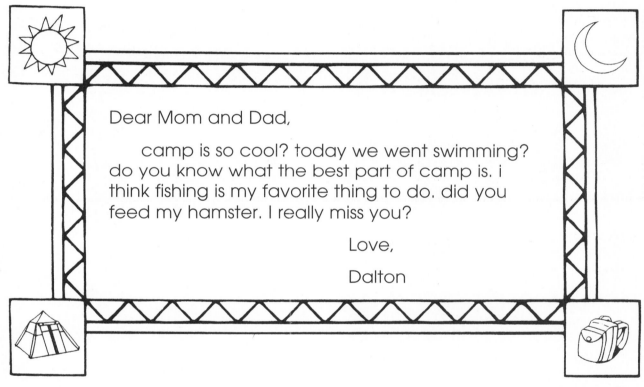

Dear Mom and Dad,

   camp is so cool? today we went swimming? do you know what the best part of camp is. i think fishing is my favorite thing to do. did you feed my hamster. I really miss you?

   Love,

   Dalton

Now choose two questions and two statements from Dalton's letter. Rewrite each correctly.

1. _____

2. _____

3. _____

4. _____

On another sheet of paper, write a letter to a friend or family member. Include two statements and two questions.

A Day at the Beach

 *A sentence that shows strong feeling or excitement is called an **exclamation**.*
*It ends with an **exclamation point** (!). For example: Look at that shark!*

Finish each sentence by putting a period, a question mark, or an exclamation point in the shell at the end.

1. I wonder if Jamie will be at the beach today

2. Did you bring the beach ball

3. Look at the size of the waves

4. Where did I leave my sunglasses

5. Mom put snacks in the beach bag

6. Watch out for that jellyfish

7. Do you want to build a sandcastle

8. The sun is bright today

9. Did you see that sailboat

10. Don't step on that starfish

11. It is windy near the seashore

12. Should we put up an umbrella

 Read these sentences: I see a sand crab. I see a sand crab! How does your voice change?

Seashore Sentences

Complete:

A _____ ends with a period.

A _____ ends with a question mark.

An _____ ends with an exclamation point.

Write a statement (S), a question (Q), and an exclamation (E) about each picture.

S _____

_____

Q _____

_____

E _____

_____

S _____

_____

Q _____

_____

E _____

_____

On another sheet of paper, write a statement, a question, and an exclamation about a picture of your choice.

Building Blocks

 A good sentence has a part that tells who or what the sentence is about. This is called the **subject**.

Make a list of possible subjects to complete each sentence.

_____ jumped the fence.

1. _____

2. _____

3. _____

_____ is too full.

1. _____

2. _____

3. _____

 A good sentence has a part that tells what happens. This is called the **action**.

Make a list of possible actions to complete each sentence.

We _____ on the playground.

1. _____

2. _____

3. _____

The cowboy _____ on his horse.

1. _____

2. _____

3. _____

 On another sheet of paper, make a list of five subjects you would like to write about.

Keep Building!

 Some sentences have a part that tells where or when the action is happening.

For each sentence, make a list of possible endings that tell where or when the action happens.

The wind blew _____.

1. _____

2. _____

3. _____

The baby tripped _____.

1. _____

2. _____

3. _____

Complete each sentence.

1. _____ made us laugh last night.

2. The door leads _____.

3. The crowd _____ at the circus.

4. The paint bucket spilled _____.

5. _____ was never seen again.

6. The firefighter _____ into the fire truck.

Get Your Ticket!

Write a sentence to match each picture. Be sure to include a subject, an action, and a part that tells where or when.

1. A boy climbs a tree in his backyard.

2. _____

3. _____

Find a comic strip. Use the pictures to write a sentence on another sheet of paper. Be sure to include a subject, an action, and a part that tells where or when.

Name _____

Slide Show

 A sentence is more interesting when it includes a subject, an action, and a part that tells where or when.

Write three sentences and draw pictures to match.

subject	action	where or when

1. _____

subject	action	where or when

2. _____

subject	action	where or when

3. _____

 Switch the sentence parts around to make three silly sentences! Write the sentences on another sheet of paper.

Mystery Bags

 Describing words *help you imagine how something looks, feels, smells, sounds, or tastes.*

Make a list of words that describe the object in each bag below.

 Use a paper sack to make a real mystery bag. Place an object in the bag and give describing clues to someone at home. Can he or she guess the mystery object?

Country Roads

 A good sentence uses describing words to help the reader "paint a picture" in his or her mind.

Add a describing word from the list to finish each sentence.

1. The _____ chicken laid

   _____ eggs in her nest.

2. The _____ barn

   keeps the _____

   animals warm at night.

3. _____ carrots grow in

   the _____ garden.

4. Two _____ pigs sleep in

   the _____ pen.

5. The _____ cows drink

   from the _____ pond.

6. A _____ scarecrow

   frightens the _____ birds.

wooden

sunny

lazy

black

three

orange

thirsty

cold

shallow

muddy

funny

fat

 On another sheet of paper, write three sentences describing your favorite place to visit.

Name _____

It's in the Bag

 Describing words *make a sentence more interesting.*

Add a describing word to each sentence.

1. My friend's _____ dog has fleas!

2. The _____ popcorn is in the big bowl.

3. How did the _____ worm get on the sidewalk?

4. The _____ ocean waves crashed against the rocks.

5. The _____ ball broke a window at school!

6. My _____ skin itched from poison ivy.

7. The two _____ squirrels chased each other up the tree.

8. The _____ sand felt good on my feet.

9. Are the _____ apples ready to be picked?

10. The _____ ball was hard to catch.

11. Is the _____ salamander hiding under the rock?

12. The _____ snow cone melted quickly.

 Ask someone at home to make a mystery bag and give you clues about the object inside.

Copyright © Scholastic Inc.

City Streets

 A good sentence uses describing words.

Write a statement (S), a question (Q), and an exclamation (E) about the picture. Use each of the following describing words:

fast   busy   crowded

S _____

_____

Q _____

_____

E _____

_____

 Describe a "mystery object" to a friend. Can he or she guess what you are describing?

Name _____

Football Frenzy

 A sentence is more interesting when it gives exact information.

Replace each word to make the sentence more exact.

1. The  game starts .

   The ___soccer___ game starts ___now___.

2. We are meeting .

   We are meeting _____ _____.

3. Let's eat  before the game.

   Let's eat _____ and _____ before

   the game.

4. I hope score points.

   I hope _____ score _____ points.

5.  were also .

   _____ were also _____.

6. 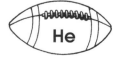 played a game!

   _____ played a _____ game!

Take Me Out to the Ball Game

 A sentence is more interesting when it gives complete information.

Finish each sentence so that it answers the  (question.)

1. The players get to the stadium  (when.)

_____

2. The team is excited because 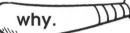 (why.)

_____

3. The fans arrive in  (what.)

_____

4. Flags are flying 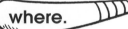 (where.)

_____

5. A man sings the "Star-Spangled Banner"  (when.)

_____

6. The fans cheer for  (whom.)

_____

7. The ball is hit (where.)

_____

 On another sheet of paper, write a sentence about your favorite game. Be sure to tell who plays the game with you.

Cake and Ice Cream

Two sentences that share the same subject can be combined to make one sentence by using the word and.

Rewrite the sentences by combining their endings.

1. The party was fun.
The party was exciting.

The party was fun and exciting.

2. We blew up orange balloons.
We blew up red balloons.

_____

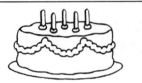 

3. We ate cake.
We ate ice cream.

_____

4. The cake frosting was green.
The cake frosting was yellow.

_____

5. We made a bookmark.
We made a clay pot.

_____

6. We brought games.
We brought prizes.

_____

Salt and Pepper

 Two sentences that share the same ending can also be combined to make one sentence.

Rewrite the sentences by combining their subjects.

1. These peanuts are salty!
   These pretzels are salty!

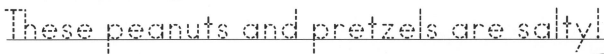

   These peanuts and pretzels are salty!

2. The first graders eat lunch at noon.
   The second graders eat lunch at noon.

   _____

3. The salt is on the counter.
   The pepper is on the counter.

   _____

4. The napkins are on the table.
   The forks are on the table.

   _____

5. Are the muffins in the oven?
   Are the cookies in the oven?

   _____

6. Michael bought lunch today.
   Stephen bought lunch today.

   _____

Great Gardening Tips

Sentences can also be combined to make them more interesting. Key words can help put two sentences together.

I will plan my garden. I am waiting for spring.

I will plan my garden while I am waiting for spring.

Combine the two sentences using the key word. Write a new sentence.

1. **Fill a cup with water. Add some flower seeds.**

   _____

2. **This will soften the seeds. They are hard.**

   _____

3. **Fill a cup with dirt. The seeds soak in water.**

   _____

4. **Bury the seeds in the cup. The dirt covers them.**

   _____

5. **Add water to the plant. Do not add too much.**

   _____

6. **Set the cup in the sun. The plant will grow.**

   _____

Growing Sentences

 Sentences can be combined to make them more interesting.

Write a combined sentence of your own. Use the given key word to help you.

1. while _I watch TV while my mom makes_
_____ lunch,_ _____

2. until _____

_____

3. because _____

_____

4. but _____

_____

5. or _____

_____

6. and _____

_____

 On another sheet of paper, write a combined sentence of your own using one of these key words: *after, before, during.*

The Sky's the Limit

➡️ *Some sentences include a list. A **comma** (,) is used to separate each item in the list.*

For example: Mrs. Jones asked the class to work on pages two, three, and four.

Fill in the blanks to make a list in each sentence. Watch for commas!

1. I ate _____ , _____ ,

   and _____ for breakfast.

2. We stayed with Grandma on _____ ,

   _____ , and _____ nights.

3. I found _____ , _____ ,

   and _____ in my party bag.

4. The boys played _____ ,

   _____ , and _____

   at summer camp.

5. The _____ , _____ ,

   and _____ ate the corn we scattered.

6. The pigs built their houses using _____ ,

   _____ , and _____ .

 **Cut a balloon shape out of paper. On one side,
list three objects that fly. On the other side,
write a sentence that lists these objects.**

Up, Up, and Away

 *Some sentences include a list. A **comma** (,) is used to separate each item in the list.*

Write a sentence that includes a list of the words that are given.

**coat
hat
gloves**

1. _____

_____

**spelling
reading
math**

2. _____

_____

**bread
peanut butter
jelly**

3. _____

_____

**birds
flowers
butterflies**

4. _____

_____

 On another sheet of paper, write a sentence that lists colors or shapes of balloons.

Out of This World

*After you write a sentence, go back and look for mistakes. This is called **proofreading** your work.*

Use the proofreading marks to correct the two mistakes in each sentence.

<u>m</u>ars = **Make a capital letter.**   (?) = **Add a question mark.**   (!) = **Add an exclamation point.**

(.) = **Add a period.**   (,) = **Add a comma.**   [ ] = **Add a word. (Write a describing word in the box.)**

1. Sometimes I can see mars Jupiter, and Saturn with my telescope.

   [ ]

2. There are ∧ stars in our galaxy

   [ ]

3. comets are ∧ pieces of ice and rock.

   [ ]

4. The sun is really a ∧ star

5. is there life on any other planet

   [ ]

6. Look at that ∧ shooting star

7. can you imagine traveling in space

   [ ]

8. i think I saw a ∧ alien.

On another sheet of paper, write two sentences about space with two mistakes in each. Ask someone at home to proofread your sentences. Is he or she correct?

Smart About Saturn

 Be sure to proofread your work.

Matthew's science report has nine mistakes. Use proofreading marks to correct his work. Then rewrite the report. Add at least two describing words to the report.

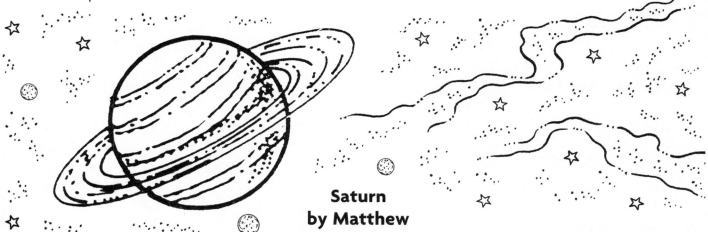

**Saturn
by Matthew**

Saturn is famous for the rings that surround it? its rings are made of ice, rock and dirt. The rings circle around the planet! Saturn is made mostly of gas? saturn's gases are lighter than water That means Saturn would float if you put it into a tub of water Saturn has more than 60 moons

_____

_____

_____

_____

_____

💡 **On another sheet of paper, write a short report about your favorite planet. Be sure to proofread it when you are done.**

Banana-Rama

Color the word that is missing from each sentence.

1. We _____ a spelling test yesterday. taked took

2. There _____ frost on the ground. was were

3. Tommy _____ the Statue of Liberty. seen saw

4. How _____ elephants are at the zoo? much many

5. Claire _____ her lizard to school. brought brang

6. Have you _____ my dog? seen saw

7. Alyssa _____ a new pair of skates. gots has

8. You _____ supposed to finish your work. are is

9. We _____ standing near a snake! were was

10. They _____ a pig in the mud. seen saw

11. We _____ our winter boots. wore weared

12. Is she _____ to come over? gonna going

13. _____ your cat climb trees? Do Does

14. Rosie _____ cookies to the bake sale. brang brought

An Apple a Day

Find the word that is incorrect in each sentence. Draw an apple around it and write the correct word on the line.

1. Laura brang a snack to camp. _____

2. I seen the sea lion show at the zoo. _____

3. Drew gots a dinosaur collection. _____

4. Mara taked her dog for a walk. _____

5. We is going to see the movie. _____

6. Jason runned to the playground. _____

7. How many pennies do you got? _____

8. The kids was having fun. _____

9. Did you saw the soccer game? _____

10. How much do that cost? _____

11. Kelly brang her cat to school! _____

12. I does my homework after school. _____

Eat an apple. Then on another sheet of paper, write a statement, a question, and an exclamation describing the apple. Be sure each sentence uses correct words.

Stories of Nature

 Sentences should be written in the correct order to tell a story.

Finish the stories by writing a sentence about each of the last two pictures.

 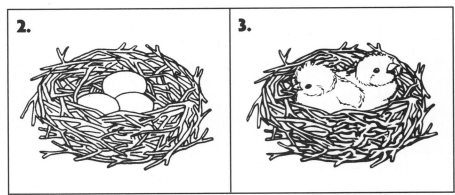

First: Two birds build a nest.

Next: _____

Last: _____

First: A flower bud grows.

Next: _____

Last: _____

Name _____

Nestled in a Nest

Write a sentence about each picture to make your own story.

_____

_____

_____

_____

_____

_____

_____

_____

_____

_____

_____

_____

 Read your story to a friend.

Stories on Parade

 *Stories have a **beginning** (B), a **middle** (M), and an **end** (E).*

Write a middle sentence that tells what happens next. Then write an ending sentence that tells what happens last.

B During the parade, five funny clowns jumped out of a purple bus.

M Next, _____

E Finally, _____

B A big balloon got loose in the wind.

M Next, _____

E Finally, _____

B A group of horses stopped right in front of us.

M Next, _____

E Finally, _____

B Some clowns were riding motorcycles.

M Next, _____

E Finally, _____

 On another sheet of paper, draw a picture of a parade that shows what is happening in the stories you wrote.

An Original Story

Choose a story idea from the list. Then write a beginning, a middle, and an ending sentence to make a story of your own. Color a picture to match each part.

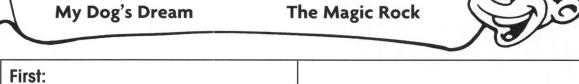

The Best Birthday Ever   **King for a Day**

My Dog's Dream   **The Magic Rock**

B

First: _____

_____

_____

_____

M

Next: _____

_____

_____

_____

E

Last: _____

_____

_____

_____

Staple three sheets of paper together to make a book. Write another story and draw a picture for each part.

Once Upon a Time

 *The **setting** of a story tells when or where it is happening.*

Imagine that you are writing a story for each picture below. How will you describe the setting? Write a sentence describing each setting.

It was a hot morning in the desert.

_____
_____
_____

_____
_____
_____

_____
_____
_____

_____
_____
_____

 On another sheet of paper, describe the setting of your favorite movie.

All Kinds of Characters

 The people or animals in a story are called **characters**.

Some characters are likable and others are not. Write a describing sentence about each character. Be sure to give each character a name.

| setting | → | characters | → | problem | → | solution |

 On another sheet of paper, make a list of four people you know well. Write three words that describe each of them. Cross out the four names and write animal names instead. Now you have four characters to use in your next story!

That's a Problem!

*To make a story exciting, one of the characters often runs into a **problem**.*

Think about each character in the sentences below. What could happen that would make a problem for that character? Write the next sentence creating a problem.

setting	→	characters	→	problem	→	solution

1. Beauty Butterfly was enjoying the warm spring day.

_____

2. Jesse was supposed to wear shoes outside.

_____

3. Gabby could not wait to bite into her apple.

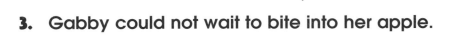

_____

4. Ben smacked the baseball into the air.

_____

5. Barney Bass had never seen such a big worm!

_____

Good Solution!

➡️ *At the end of a story, the problem is usually solved. This is called the **solution**.*

Read the beginning and middle parts of the stories below. Write an ending solution for each.

setting	→	characters	→	problem	→	solution

David and his dog, Spot, were best friends. They went everywhere together. At bedtime, David whistled for Spot to jump in his bed. One winter night, David whistled and whistled, but Spot did not come.

_____

_____

_____

Josh loved second grade, but he did not like recess. Josh's class was always the last one out to the playground. Every day, Josh ran to get a swing, but they were always taken.

_____

_____

_____

 On another sheet of paper, make a list of three problems you have faced. How did you solve each problem?

The Mighty Knight

 A **story map** *helps you plan the setting, characters, problem, and solution.*

Write a sentence about each part of the map to make a story.

_____

_____

_____

_____

_____

_____

_____

_____

Read your story to a friend.

A Story Fit for a King

Use a story map to help plan your story before you begin writing.

Complete the map. Then use it to write a story "fit for a king."

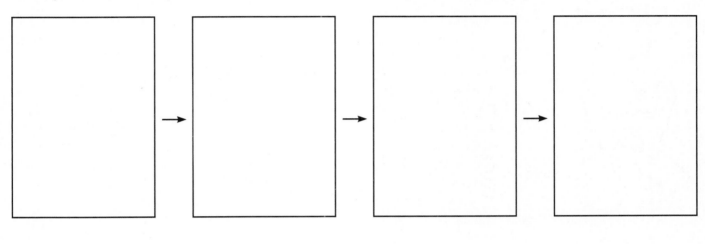

_____

_____

_____

_____

_____

_____

_____

_____

Turn your story into a puppet show! Perform your puppet show for someone at home.

The Father of Our Country

After you finish writing, go back and look for mistakes.

Use the proofreading marks to correct eight mistakes in the letter.

m̲ars = **Make a capital letter.**   ? = **Add a question mark.**   ! = **Add an exclamation point.**

. = **Add a period.**   , = **Add a comma.**

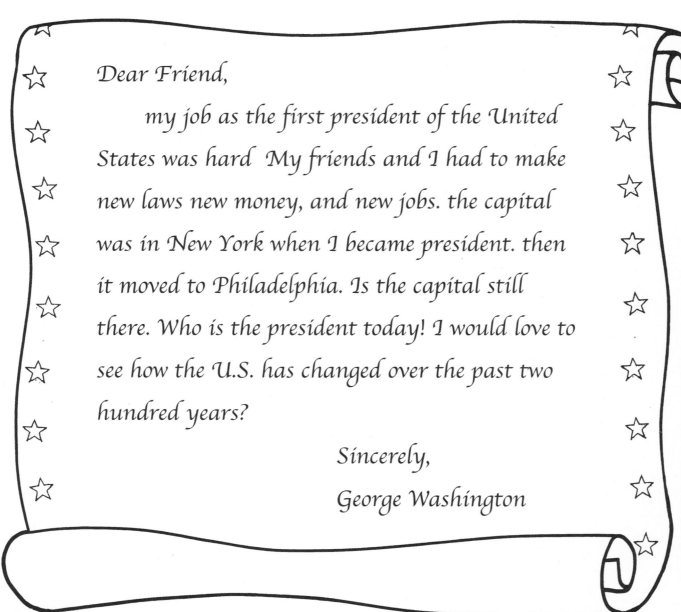

Dear Friend,

　　　my job as the first president of the United States was hard My friends and I had to make new laws new money, and new jobs. the capital was in New York when I became president. then it moved to Philadelphia. Is the capital still there. Who is the president today! I would love to see how the U.S. has changed over the past two hundred years?

　　　　　　　　　　Sincerely,

　　　　　　　　　　George Washington

On another sheet of paper, write a letter to today's president. The White House address is: 1600 Pennsylvania Avenue Washington, D.C. 20500.

Presidential Pen Pals

A **friendly letter** *has five parts: the date, greeting, body, closing, and signature.*

Use the five parts to write a letter back to George Washington. Be sure to proofread your work for mistakes.

_____
(today's date)

_____,
(greeting)

_____
(body)
_____

_____

_____

_____

_____

_____

_____

_____,
(closing)

_____
(your name)

Page 4
Many of; Our teacher; The reading; The globe; We study; Our class

Page 5
1. Art class; 2. Today we; 3. First, we; 4. The next; 5. My teacher; 6. Next week

Page 6
1. The blue whale is the largest animal in the world. 2. Even dinosaurs were not as large as the blue whale. 3. Blue whales are not part of the fish family. 4. The blue whale has no teeth. 5. Blue whales eat tiny sea creatures. 6. Blue whales have two blowholes.

Page 7
Sentences will vary.

Page 8
1. Where is the king's castle? 2. Who helped Humpty Dumpty? 3. Why did the cow jump over the moon? 4. Will the frog become a prince? 5. Could the three mice see?

Page 9
Sentences will vary.

Page 10
1. .; 2. ?; 3. ?; 4. .; 5. ?; 6. .; 7. ?; 8. .

Page 11
1. The sun is the closest star to Earth. 2. The sun is not the brightest star. 3. What is the temperature of the sun? 4. The sun is a ball of hot gas. 5. How large is the sun? 6. Will the sun ever burn out?

Page 12
Sentences will vary.

Page 13
Dear Mom and Dad,
    Camp is so cool! Today we went swimming. Do you know what the best part of camp is? I think fishing is my favorite thing to do. Did you feed my hamster? I really miss you.
Love, Dalton

Sentences will vary.

Page 14
1. .; 2. ?; 3. !; 4. ?; 5. .; 6. !; 7. ?; 8. .; 9. ?; 10. !; 11. .; 12. ?

Page 15
Sentences will vary.

Page 16
Answers will vary.

Page 17
Answers will vary.

Page 18
Sentences may vary. Possible answers: 1. A boy climbs a tree in his backyard. 2. A cat plays with fish in the living room. 3. A bunny eats a carrot in the garden.

Page 19
Sentences and pictures will vary.

Page 20
Lists of words will vary.

Page 21
Answers will vary. 1. fat, three; 2. wooden, cold; 3. Orange, sunny; 4. lazy, muddy; 5. thirsty, shallow; 6. funny, black

Page 22
Describing words will vary.

Page 23
Sentences will vary.

Page 24
Sentences will vary.

Page 25
Sentences will vary.

Page 26
1. The party was fun and exciting. 2. We blew up orange and red balloons. 3. We ate cake and ice cream. 4. The cake frosting was green and yellow. 5. We made a bookmark and a clay pot. 6. We brought games and prizes.

Page 27
1. These peanuts and pretzels are salty. 2. The first graders and second graders eat lunch at noon. 3. The salt and pepper are on the counter.

4. The napkins and forks are on the table. 5. Are the muffins and cookies in the oven? 6. Michael and Stephen bought lunch today.

Page 28
1. Fill a cup with water and add some flower seeds. 2. This will soften the seeds because they are hard. 3. Fill a cup with dirt while the seeds soak in water. 4. Bury the seeds in the cup until the dirt covers them. 5. Add water to the plant but do not add too much. 6. Set the cup in the sun so the plant will grow.

Page 29
Sentences will vary.

Page 30
Answers will vary.

Page 31
Sentences will vary.

Page 32
Describing words will vary.
1. Sometimes I can see Mars, Jupiter, and Saturn with my telescope. 2. There are many stars in our galaxy. 3. Comets are large pieces of ice and rock. 4. The sun is really a huge star. 5. Is there life on any other planet? 6. Look at that beautiful shooting star! 7. Can you imagine traveling in space? 8. I think I saw a little alien.

Page 33
Describing words will vary.

Saturn is famous for the rings that surround it. Its rings are made of ice, rock, and dirt. The rings circle around the planet. Saturn is made mostly of gas. Saturn's gases are lighter than water. That means Saturn would float if you put it into a tub of water. Saturn has more than 60 moons.

Page 34
1. took; 2. was; 3. saw; 4. many; 5. brought; 6. seen; 7. has; 8. are; 9. were; 10. saw; 11. wore; 12. going; 13. Does; 14. brought

Page 35
1. ~~brang~~, brought; 2. ~~seen~~, saw; 3. ~~gots~~, has; 4. ~~taked~~, took; 5. ~~is~~, are; 6. ~~runned~~, ran; 7. ~~got~~, have; 8. ~~was~~, were; 9. ~~saw~~, see; 10. ~~do~~, does; 11. ~~brang~~, brought; 12. ~~does~~, do

Page 36
Sentences will vary.

Page 37
Sentences will vary.

Page 38
Sentences will vary.

Page 39
Stories will vary.

Page 40
Sentences will vary.

Page 41
Sentences will vary.

Page 42
Sentences will vary.

Page 43
Answers will vary.

Page 44
Stories will vary.

Page 45
Stories will vary.

Page 46
Dear Friend,
    My job as the first president of the United States was hard. My friends and I had to make new laws, new money, and new jobs. The capital was in New York when I became president. Then it moved to Philadelphia. Is the capital still there? Who is the president today? I would love to see how the U.S. has changed over the past two hundred years!
Sincerely,
George Washington

Page 47
Letters will vary.